IMAGES
of America

Maison Blanche Department Stores

I0792592

Mr. Bingle in the Oaks. This large Mr. Bingle figure once looked down on Canal Street from the front of the flagship store of the Maison Blanche chain. Since November 2005, this Bingle is part of the "Celebration in the Oaks" display presented annually at City Park. (Author.)

On the Cover: The "MB Building," 1909. The Old Opera House (the structure adjacent to the Mercier Building, the original Maison Blanche) has been torn down, but its replacement, the Audubon Building, has not yet been constructed. The entrance portico on the left side (Rue Burgundy) of the building led to the upper floors of the office towers. The sign on the building to the right of the MB towers informs the public that it has been purchased by the Chas. A. Kaufman Co., Ltd. Prior to 1901, this company used to be named the Kaufman-Isaacs Co., but Mark Isaacs joined S.J. Shwartz to operate Maison Blanche. This building later became a Katz & Besthoff Drug Store. (Library of Congress.)

IMAGES
of America

MAISON BLANCHE DEPARTMENT STORES

Edward J. Branley

ARCADIA
PUBLISHING

ISBN 978-0-7385-8817-9

Published by Arcadia Publishing
Charleston, South Carolina

Printed in the United States of America

Library of Congress Control Number: 2011929089

For all general information, please contact Arcadia Publishing:
Telephone 843-853-2070
Fax 843-853-0044
E-mail sales@arcadiapublishing.com
For customer service and orders:
Toll-Free 1-888-313-2665

Visit us on the Internet at www.arcadiapublishing.com

To my wife, Helen, whom I met and dated while I was a student at the University of New Orleans in the late 1970s. I paid for the wonderful times we had while going out by working nights at Maison Blanche Clearview.

Helen, I love you.

Contents

ACKNOWLEDGMENTS

Thanks to Amy Perryman, my acquisitions editor at Arcadia, for her guidance and advice. You are the best.

Thanks to Jennifer Lloyd, George "Loki" Williams IV, Anthony "Turducken" DelRosario, Carlos "Infrogmation" May, Joe Hollier, Jeffery Kent, Louis Maistros, Pat Jolly, Liz Simoneaux Dorsey, and Tess Conrad for assistance in hunting down and providing photographs, and thanks to Brother Neal Golden, SC, for fact-checking assistance. Thanks to Char Thian, Ritz-Carlton, New Orleans, for hotel background. Special thanks to Ryan J. Bordenave of the New Orleans Downtown Development District for sharing his wealth of knowledge on Canal Street, its buildings, and their architecture.

All my love to my wife, Helen, and my sons, Justin and Kevin, for putting up with me during the project. A huge thank you to Jenifer Hill Akers for unique skills in keeping me sane. Thanks to the Special Collections staff at the Earl K. Long Library, University of New Orleans. Irene Wainwright, archivist, Louisiana Collection, New Orleans Public Library, and her staff were wonderful to work with once again. Special thanks to the folks at the PJ's Coffee Shops in Clearview Mall and by the University of New Orleans for giving me wonderful work environments to escape to. A big hug of appreciation goes to my Yatmedia business partner, Greta Perry, for putting up with the distractions.

Photographs are credited using abbreviations: New Orleans Public Library (NOPL), Earl K. Long Library, University of New Orleans (UNO), Library of Congress (LOC), and Edward J. Branley (Author).

INTRODUCTION

The story of Maison Blanche is a reflection of the city the store served. Jewish emigrants from Germany had been coming to Southeast Louisiana since the 1820s. That community was well established with financiers and merchants by the beginning of the war. These merchants and others recognized early on that Canal Street, with its 140-foot width (a navigation canal was actually planned for the middle of the street but never materialized), would be a major thoroughfare and began to invest in real estate along this, the boundary between the Vieux Carré (the "old square") and Faubourg Ste. Marie (the "American Quarter"). Since the 1830s, streetcars and steam trains brought people from Uptown to Canal Street, and Canal got its own street railway line in 1861. The stage was set for a postwar economic boom.

One of the merchants making a good living on Canal Street was Abraham Shwartz, who operated a dry goods store. Some say the stress of dealing with the fire that destroyed the family store in 1892 contributed to his death that year. His son Simon left the family business after his father passed, opening his own dry goods store in the 900 block of Canal Street. Shwartz joined another prominent local family when he married banker Isidore Newman's daughter. Shwartz's vision for expanding his business, along with his father-in-law's wealth, enabled him to convert the dry goods store into New Orleans's first department store.

The Maison Blanche (MB) quickly became a go-to place to shop on Canal Street, and the five floors of the Mercier Building in the 900 block bustled with customers and profit. Shwartz's vision and ambition did not stop here, though. He demolished his store in stages, starting in 1907. In its place, he constructed the largest building in the city at the time, a structure with 13 stories, the first 5 of which were a massive retail area. This new Maison Blanche opened in 1909, along with eight floors of office space above the store. The building gave solid backing to Shwartz's advertising slogan for MB, the "Greatest Store South." When expansions to the building were completed in 1958, Maison Blanche on Canal Street offered 565,000 square feet of retail space.

In 1922, the Shwartz and Newman families merged Maison Blanche into City Stores, Inc., a Philadelphia-based investment group. City Stores merged MB with Loveman's of Birmingham, Alabama, and B. Lowenstein's of Memphis, Tennessee. Maison Blanche's unique New Orleans style had a significant impact on the parent company, including the eventual rise of Isidore Newman II, the patriarch's grandson, to the presidency of City Stores.

After 50 years of operation as a single-store business, Maison Blanche branched out, opening stores in Gentilly (at Gentilly Road and Elysian Fields) and in Mid City (at Carrollton and Tulane Avenues) in 1947. Expansion continued in the 1950s, with new stores opening in Metairie (Airline Village) and on the West Bank (Westside). Maison Blanche opened its first mall stores in the 1960s: Gentilly Woods in 1961 and Clearview (Metairie) in 1969. With the opening of stores in the Plaza in Lake Forest (New Orleans East), North Shore Square (Slidell, Louisiana), and Bon Marche Mall (Baton Rouge, Louisiana), the chain's expansion reached its peak in the mid-1970s. In the 1990s, Goudchaux's closed MB Westside, opening a store in the newly remodeled Oakwood Shopping Center, also in Gretna.

City Stores owned and operated Maison Blanche until the company went bankrupt in 1979. Attempts at reorganization over the next three years were unsuccessful, and Maison Blanche was sold to Goudchaux's of Baton Rouge, which was owned by the Sternberg family. The Canal Street building was sold off by City Stores in a separate transaction, so that store closed. Goudchaux's (not to be confused with the Leon Godchaux Co. of New Orleans) operated the suburban stores as Goudchaux–Maison Blanche.

The Sternbergs continued to grow their chain, acquiring department stores in other cities during the 1980s. In 1991, they sold their holdings to Cincinnati-based Mercantile Stores. The new owners dropped the Goudchaux's name, operating once again as just Maison Blanche. Mercantile Stores was, in turn, acquired by Dillard's of Little Rock, Arkansas, in 1998. Dillard's converted the stores to their name and brand, closing the Canal Street store and other locations where there were already Dillard's stores. After over 100 years, the Maison Blanche brand ceased to exist.

In addition to the landmark building on Canal Street, another Maison Blanche icon continues to leave a lasting impression on New Orleans. In 1947, MB introduced a new Christmas character, "Mr. Bingle," to the world. The little snow fairy, with his holly wings and ice-cream-cone hat, quickly won the hearts of New Orleanians, becoming the most recognizable Christmas symbol in the city. The Mr. Bingle character was created by MB's display director, Emile Alline. Alline, in turn, hired puppeteer Edwin Harmon "Oscar" Isentrout to operate a Bingle marionette and be the character's voice. When MB was acquired by Mercantile Stores, Mr. Bingle's reach extended from New Orleans to as far away as Fargo, North Dakota, as the Christmas mascot of deLendrecies. Mr. Bingle lives on as a Christmas mascot of Dillard's, while Bingle lore and traditions continue in the wider New Orleans community.

The Canal Street store was not part of the 1982 transaction between City Stores and Goudchaux's. The Sternbergs leased three floors of Canal Street from the new owners and reopened the downtown store in 1984, but it was a shadow of its former self. The building was sold once again in 1997, and the owners announced plans to convert it and the S.H. Kress building next door into a hotel. Hopes that MB would continue to operate on the first floor of the hotel were dashed when Dillard's acquired the MB chain. In 2000, the Ritz Carlton, New Orleans, opened and continues to operate in those two buildings today.

As local musician Benny Grunch would say, Maison Blanche "ain't dere no more," but the stores live on in the memories of former employees and customers alike. With the big Mr. Bingle on display every Christmas at City Park and Dillard's using Mr. Bingle as their mascot, the initials *MB* continue to be a part of New Orleans culture.

One

Simon Shwartz's Canal Street

The conventional wisdom in New Orleans is that Isidore Newman founded Maison Blanche. That distinction actually belongs to his son-in-law. It is better to say that Newman *funded* MB.

Following the devastating fire that destroyed his father's dry goods store, Simon J. Shwartz Sr. struck out on his own, opening S.J. Shwartz and Co. in the Mercier Building located at Canal Street and Rue Dauphine. Shwartz operated the dry goods store for four years when he announced plans to convert the business into a full-blown department store, the first of its kind in New Orleans. With financial backing from father-in-law, Isidore Newman, Shwartz remodeled the Mercier Building and opened the Maison Blanche on October 30, 1897. The store operated for 10 years in the Mercier Building, gaining in popularity and inspiring others to open department stores on Canal Street. Not satisfied with the growth potential of the Mercier Building, Shwartz planned to erect a five-story retail store on the site of the Maison Blanche, adding another eight stories above the retail area for office space. The construction plan was designed to keep the store open throughout the process, creating a bigger and better Maison Blanche by 1909.

Canal Street, Mid-1880s. This is an artist's rendering of an 1880s photograph of Canal Street. The massive statue in the middle is the Henry Clay Monument. All the streetcars in this illustration are mule-drawn. Rising above the street in the back is the domed cupola of the Mercier Building. (NOPL.)

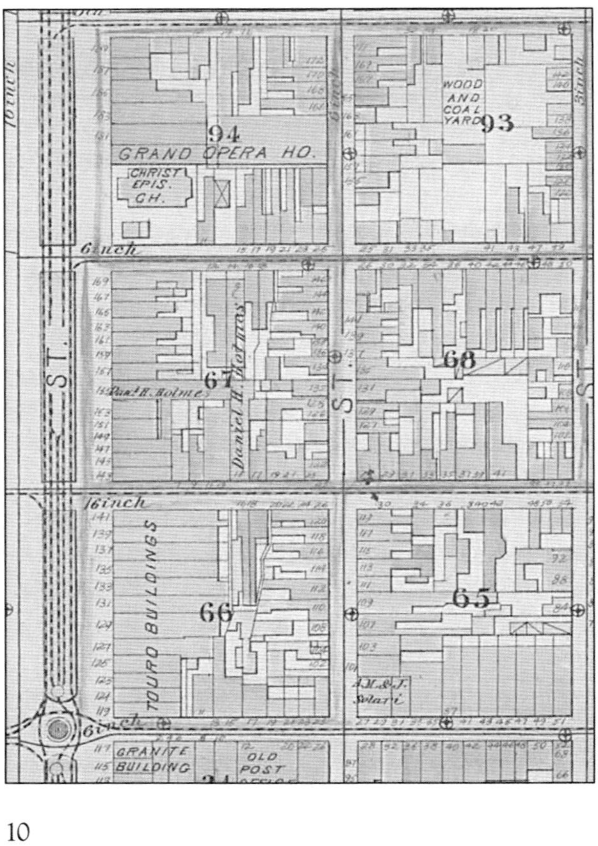

Setting the Stage. This portion of the *Robinson Street Atlas* from 1880 shows the 700, 800, and 900 blocks of Canal Street on the French Quarter side. The chapter of Christ Church Episcopal sold their property located at Canal Street and Rue Dauphine at auction in May 1885. The church and rectory were demolished, and D. Mercier built a five-story building on the lot. Mercier did not move his dry goods business into the Canal Street building, preferring to lease it out to other companies. Sections of the 800 block are marked, "Daniel Henry Holmes." The D.H. Holmes department store was a competitor to Maison Blanche, in both business and for the hearts of New Orleanians. (Clerk of Civil Court, City of New Orleans.)

Oldest Parish. Christ Church is shown in the late 1870s. The first Christ Church was a block down, on Canal Street and Rue Bourbon (better known as Bourbon Street). That building was sold to Judah Touro, and the proceeds enabled the vestry to acquire the corner of Canal Street and Rue Dauphine. By the 1880s, this was prime retail and hotel real estate, so the vestry voted to sell it and move uptown to St. Charles Avenue and Seventh Street. The new Uptown church became Christ Church Cathedral, the seat of the Episcopal Diocese of Louisiana. (LOC.)

STREET LEVEL. Canal Street is seen here in the late 1880s from the Clay Monument located in the middle of the median (known to locals as "neutral ground") at St. Charles Avenue. Mule-drawn "bobtail" streetcars fill the neutral ground, and the Mercier Building dominates the background. (NOPL.)

Looking up Canal. Wilson S. Howell shot this photograph on March 15, 1890, at 3:45 p.m. The image was taken from one block farther down than the shot on the previous page, with the Clay Monument is visible. Judah Touro purchased the original Christ Church property in the 700 block of Canal Street to erect the row of buildings on the right. (NOPL.)

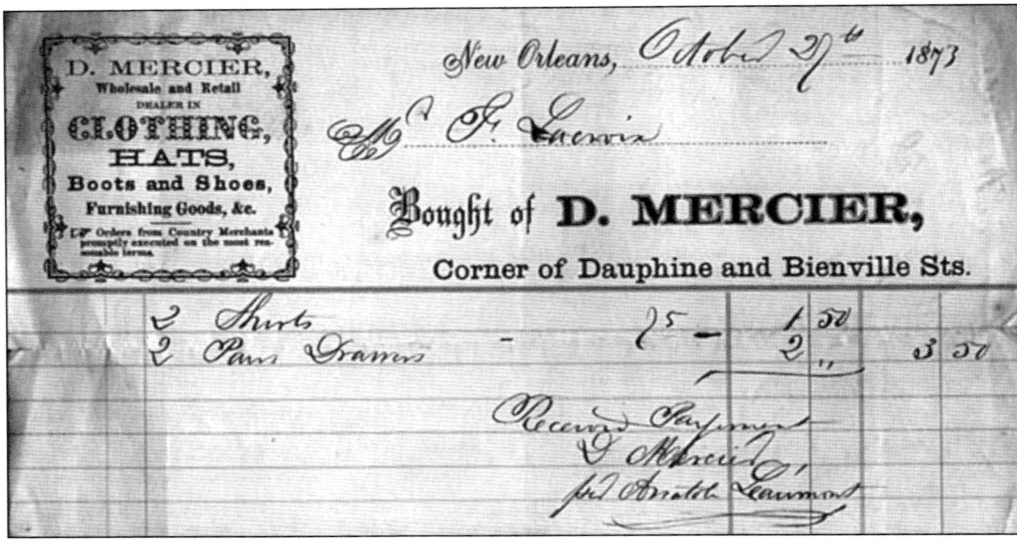

D. MERCIER,
Wholesale and Retail
DEALER IN
CLOTHING,
HATS,
Boots and Shoes,
Furnishing Goods, &c.
Orders from Country Merchants promptly executed on the most reasonable terms.

New Orleans, October 27th 1873

Mr F. Lacroix

Bought of D. MERCIER,
Corner of Dauphine and Bienville Sts.

2 Shirts	75	1 50		
2 Pairs Drawers		2 "		3 50

Received Payment
D. Mercier
per Anatole Laumont

NEW ORLEANS DRY GOODS STORES. Above is a receipt for the purchase of two shirts and two pairs of "drawers" from D. Mercier, located two blocks away from Canal Street in the French Quarter. The Mercier Building, at 901 Canal Street, was originally leased to L. Fellman & Co., and later to S.J. Shwartz & Co. At left, is a New Orleans item advertisement for the grand opening of S.J. Shwartz & Co. on October 17, 1892. (Both, NOPL.)

BANKER, PHILANTHROPIST, PATRIARCH. Isidore Newman (1836–1909) left his home in Kaiserslautern, in what was then Rhenish Bavaria, at the age of 17 to come to Louisiana. By 1877, he was a successful investment banker with an office on Carondelet Street in the heart of the city's financial district. One of Newman's best investments was in his son-in-law's career, staking S.J. Shwartz and his plan to open Maison Blanche. (Both, NOPL.)

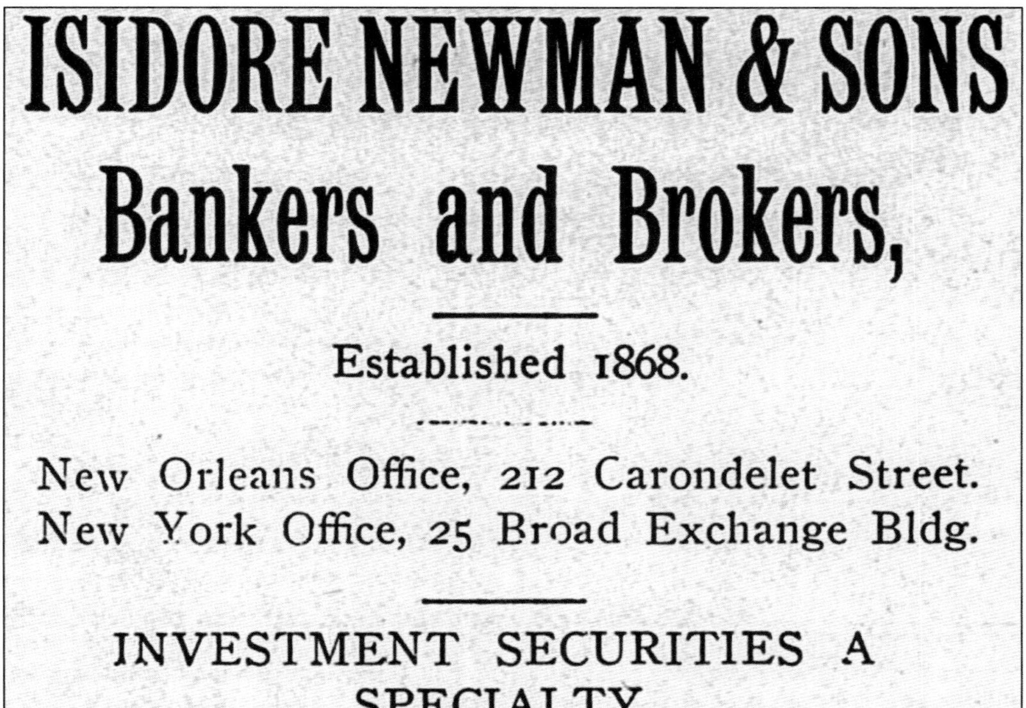

Remodeling the Mercier Building. Already occupying the building at Canal Street and Rue Dauphine, Shwartz's ambition was to convert his dry goods business into a full-blown department store. The plan was to call the new store the Maison Blanche, or "White House," and to make it the most attractive retail establishment in New Orleans. (Both, NOPL.)

SHWARTZ'S CANAL STREET. The Mercier Building (center-left) rules over the chaos of electric wires, streetcars, and horse- and mule-drawn wagons in the 800 and 900 blocks of Canal Street. This stereoscopic photograph, captioned "Canal St., the main thoroughfare of New Orleans," was shot in about 1901. (LOC.)

THE BRAIN TRUST. Isidore Newman's son-in-law S.J. Shwartz, his brother-in-law Gus Schulhoefer, and his son Hartwig Newman were the first management team of Maison Blanche, shown here from a profile piece in the *New Orleans Picayune* in 1897. (UNO.)

THE MAISON BLANCHE. Shwartz, with funding from his father-in-law, converted the Mercier Building into a retail palace, opening the city's first department store on October 31, 1897. The main entrance was located on the corner of Canal and Dauphine Streets. Several Brill and Ford, Bacon & Davis single-truck streetcars pass in front of the grand store. (NOPL.)

Management Changes. By 1901, Gus Schulhoefer had passed away, and Hart Newman moved from Maison Blanche to his father's Carondelet Street banking firm. S.J. Shwartz brought local retailer Marks Isaacs in, renaming the company that operated the Maison Blanche to the Shwartz & Isaacs Co., Ltd. Isaacs would later leave Maison Blanche to open his own department store in the 700 block of Canal Street. (NOPL.)

Transit Hub. This Alexander Allison photograph of the 900 block of Canal Street, looking toward the river, was shot around 1905. Streetcars and wagons demonstrate Canal Street's role as the main thoroughfare of New Orleans. The smoke in the photograph is most likely from steam trains running out to West End and Spanish Fort. The Grand Opera House is visible just to the left of Maison Blanche. (NOPL.)

Night Advertising. This Teunisson photograph from 1898 shows the popularity of electric advertising signs, which are strung across the tracks on Canal Street. Signs advertising the West End entertainment area at Lake Pontchartrain and the Greenwall Theater are visible in front of Maison Blanche. (NOPL.)

Expansion Plans. Not content with the retail space available in the Mercier Building, Shwartz planned to demolish the five-story structure, replacing it with a much taller building. An early conceptual sketch was published by the *Picayune* in 1905, along with an article describing the store's plan. (UNO.)

Under Construction. This Alexander Allison photograph of Mardi Gras 1907 shows that construction of the new Maison Blanche is well under way. Shwartz's plan was to demolish the Rue Iberville side of the Mercier Building first, keeping the Canal Street side open for business during construction. The first five floors of the new building were to be retail space, with eight additional stories in two towers for office space. Allison shot this photograph from the Morris Building. (NOPL.)

Two

Greatest Store South

The original Maison Blanche located in the Mercier Building continued to operate while the new Maison Blanche building was erected behind it. When the rear of the building was complete, the front portion of the old structure was demolished, and the store operated with an entrance on Rue Iberville and Rue Dauphine. At the time, the finished building was the tallest in the city. It was not long before "MB Canal" became a New Orleans landmark, offering quality merchandise and friendly service. The store survived the bankruptcy of parent company City Stores in 1979. The holding company closed the store in 1982, but it was reopened in 1984 when the MB chain was sold to Goudchaux's of Baton Rouge. Goudchaux's subsequently sold the MB locations to Dillard's, and that company permanently closed the Canal Street location.

Maison Blanche

LIMITED.

We Are Moving

TO

"Greater Maison Blanche"

Get Acquainted With the New Canal Street Entrance and Arcade

The store adjoining "Maison Blanche" on Canal street has been transformed into an arcade, leading to that part of "Greater Maison Blanche" now almost ready for occupancy and in which we will continue business until the completion of the **SOUTH'S GREATEST BUILDING.**

SHELVING AND FIXTURES are now being erected in the new building—every preparation is being made for the final move—and before this month is ended the entire community will be invited to visit us in

"GREATER MAISON BLANCHE"

UNTIL THAT DAY

Bargains In Every Department

OPEN FOR BUSINESS. When the rear portion of the new building was completed, the Maison Blanche moved into that space, and the remainder of the Mercier Building was demolished. Regular advertisements in the newspapers kept shoppers abreast of the changes in traffic flow, as entrances to the store alternated between Canal Street, Rue Iberville, Rue Dauphine, and Canal Street again. (NOPL.)

DOMINATING THE SKYLINE. Another Allison photograph from Mardi Gras 1907 shows the steel structure of the new MB building rising over the 600, 700, and 800 blocks of Canal Street. Until the construction of the Texaco building in the 1960s, the MB building was the tallest on the French Quarter side of Canal Street. (NOPL.)

Canal Street Icon. The new Maison Blanche store is shown as generations of New Orleanians and decades of visitors remember it. To the immediate left of MB, the Grand Opera House has been demolished, but the S.H. Kress building has not yet begun to be constructed, dating this photograph to 1909. The Audubon Building is visible after the empty space. The home of Maison Blanche was now the first five floors of the new building. Those floors extend from Canal Street, down the entire block, and back to Rue Iberville. (LOC.)

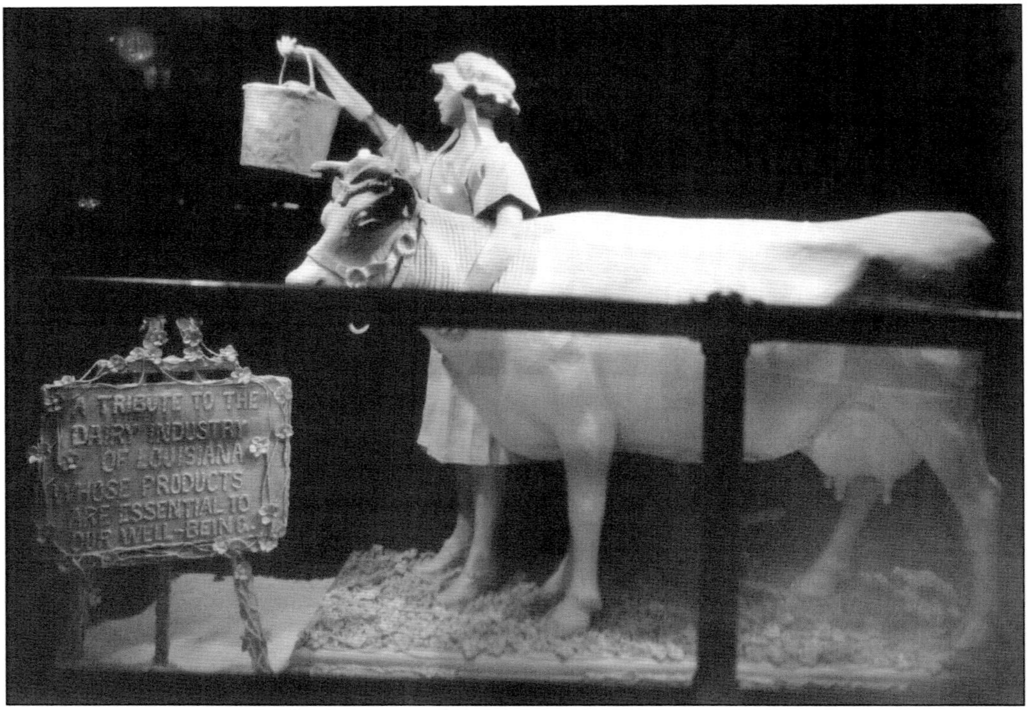

THE BUTTER COW. A 1921 clipping in a scrapbook read: "The Butter Cow. This sculptured butter cow was made by J.E. Wallace Lincoln [*sic*], Nebraska, in one of Maison Blanche's large windows. The large iron bar across the window shown in the picture was placed there to prevent to [*sic*] crowds from crushing the plate window. The exhibit attracted more attention than any other connected with the milk campaign. Mr. Wallace used 400 pounds of butter in modelling this cow and girl and about 1500 pounds of ice per day were consumed to keep the window refrigerated." Below is a shot of the crowd viewing the Butter Cow. (Both, NOPL.)

SAENGER–MAISON BLANCHE RADIO. Above, a postcard from the late 1920s shows the twin transmission towers that were constructed on the roof of the MB building in 1925, marking the beginning of WSMB Radio, AM 1360. The call letters reflect the partnership between the Saenger Theater, located on Canal and Rampart Streets, and Maison Blanche, two blocks down from the theater. At right is a full-page advertisement that ran on Sunday, April 19, 1925, announcing the opening of the radio station and the selling of radios to enjoy its programming. (Both, NOPL.)

Modernization. The first escalator in New Orleans was installed at MB on Canal Street in 1921. (NOPL.)

Transit Strike. The Canal Street neutral ground should be filled with streetcars, but the motormen and conductors of New Orleans Public Service, Inc., went on strike July 2, 1929. A summer and fall of no public transit was hard on Canal Street retailers relying on the streetcars to get people downtown. (UNO.)

Looking Down. Alexander Allison shot this photograph from one of the upper-floor offices of the Maison Blanche building around 1910. He is looking down at the intersection of Canal (foreground) and Baronne Streets. The building on the right is the Chess, Checkers, and Whist Club. That corner is now occupied by a Walgreens drugstore. (NOPL.)

Bargain Shopping. A 1926 advertisement announces that the cash-only policy of the Budget Annex located directly behind the main store would be abolished on April 1. Charge customers would be allowed to use their credit. The Budget Annex, along with the "budget stores" across town, offered shoppers the opportunity to purchase MB merchandise at deeply discounted prices. (UNO.)

Fires! Fire is always a concern for any business owner. Maison Blanche was no stranger to fires at the Canal Street store. At left, this advertisement from the *Times-Picayune* announces the reopening of the store on July 21, 1935, after a very serious fire on June 18. MB held, of course, a fire sale. (NOPL.)

Across the Street. This is a view of the MB building from the Chess, Checkers, and Whist Club on the other side of Canal Street around 1925. The French Quarter is visible behind the store. (LOC.)

War Effort. Just as they had for World War I, the management and employees of Maison Blanche supported the war effort during World War II with displays like this massive appeal to buy war bonds in 1942. (LOC.)

Snacks! This Gulledge photograph from the 1940s shows the building immediately behind Maison Blanche at the corner of Rue Dauphine and Rue Iberville. The building was owned by the store and housed the MB Snack Store, which sold bakery items. (NOPL.)

The Shopping District. These two Detroit Publishing photographs are from 1911 and 1916. Left, pipes for belowground sewer repairs are visible in the Canal Street neutral ground. Below, a busy shopping day is captured, showing Canal Street full of streetcars, automobiles, horse-drawn wagons, bicycles, and pedestrians. (Both, LOC.)

DOWN CANAL. This view from 1958 shows Saenger Theater in the left foreground, but the MB building still rules the Canal Street skyline. Canal Street continues to evolve: the streetcar tracks in the neutral ground are down to two because of the transition to buses for most routes. (NOPL.)

SPORTS! Shown are the ladies of MB softball in a local girls' league. Pictured from left to right are (first row) Jackie Sanchez, Paulette Chandler, Darlene Bayle, and Freda Ally; (second row) Peggy Dixon, Linda Links, Cynthia Bodelheimer, and Rose Loupe; (third row) Norma Garner, Leila Breaux, Tony Cinquemano (coach), Jackie Harris, and Danna Johnson. (NOPL.)

MB PHARMACY. Given the number of doctors, dentists, and optometrists who had offices in the two office towers above Maison Blanche's Canal Street retail space, it was only logical that the store would operate a pharmacy on the fifth floor. This January 1964 photograph shows three unidentified pharmacists hard at work, filling prescriptions. (NOPL.)

GIFT WRAP. Another group of employees that was busy year-round—and just crazy during the Christmas season—was the store's gift-wrap department, as seen in this November 1964 photograph of unidentified customers choosing paper while the ladies wrap it all up. (NOPL.)

"Mr. Buster Brown." Jack Ponsetti is photographed for a profile in *Shop Talk*, the employee newsletter. Ponsetti started in shoe sales, eventually moving up to buyer for men's shoes, in spite of suffering from polio. In the late 1960s, Ponsetti left MB to open his own store in Clearview Mall in Metairie. In addition to carrying the Buster Brown brand of children's shoes, Ponsetti's store sold official uniform shoes for many of the area's private and Catholic schools. (NOPL.)

Madonna. Artisans from several countries plied their crafts in the store's Grand Tour promotion of 1965. A German woodworker carved a Madonna-and-child statue for the 1965 World Tour. To determine what would be done with the statue at the end of the promotion, management held an employee raffle. The winner was allowed to choose which institution in town would receive the statue. The customer asked to draw the winning ticket, Myrtle Buhler, poses with the winner, Sylvester Monnin of the credit department. Monnin donated the statue to St. Aloysius High School on Esplanade Avenue. (NOPL.)

CAROLYN PARK. On September 9, 1965, this Chalmette neighborhood, home to several MB families, was inundated by 8 to 10 feet of floodwater as Hurricane Betsy, a category 3 storm, made landfall in Southeast Louisiana. The Canal Street store received minor damage, but the Carrollton, Airline, and Gentilly Woods stores lost all their front windows. (NOPL.)

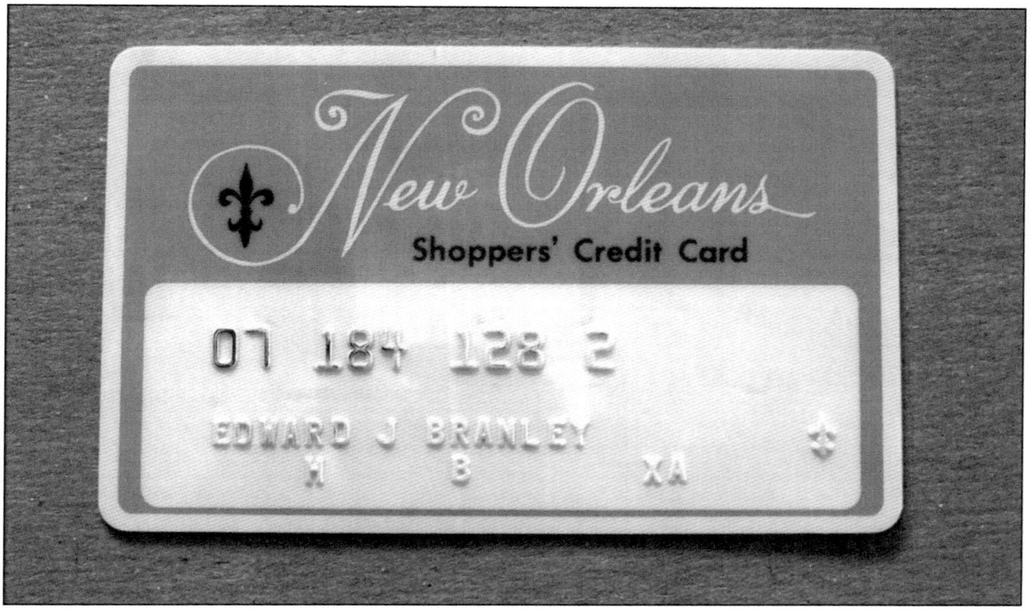

Credit Cards. Before bank cards became popular, the merchants of Canal Street organized to create a single credit-card system for their stores. This is the author's New Orleans Shoppers' Credit Card. The *H* and *B* stamped into the card indicate the holder has accounts at D.H. Holmes and Maison Blanche. Additionally, Gus Mayer, Godchaux's, and Labiche's participated in the system. (Author.)

Charge Approvals. When a shopper purchased items costing more than $25, the sales associate would have to call for approval. In April 1965, long before personal computers, the credit department manned desks on the fifth floor, and workers would walk over to the credit files, while on the line with the sales floor, to review the customer's record. (NOPL.)

ON SPECIAL. A 1950 advertisement touts some of the delicacies sold in the MB Snack Shop building at the corner of Rue Dauphine and Rue Iberville. This building was demolished in 1958, and the store building was extended all the way back to Rue Iberville. (NOPL.)

PHOTOGRAPHY. Like most major department stores, Maison Blanche had a portrait studio. Located on the fifth floor, the studio offered photograph and framing services. (NOPL.)

Renovations. The fifth floor at Canal Street underwent extensive renovations in 1965. Above, a construction crew works on the personnel department. Below is the new reception area for personnel. (Both, NOPL.)

Commercial Athletic Association Softball. The 1969 girls' softball team received a crushing 6-0 defeat at the hands of the Genuine Parts team in the league championship game. The team members are, from left to right, (first row) left fielder Ruby Spiess, third baseman Sylvia Thibodeaux, pitcher Marie St. Philip, and shortstop Jo Ann Daigle; (second row) right fielder Pat Felger, second baseman Jean Reinhardt, first baseman Sue Klein, and catcher Louise Conner; (third row) coach Paul Daigle, center fielder Leslie Blanchard, third baseman Gerri Bergeron, short fielder Freda Ally, and assistant coach Charley Henry. (NOPL.)

Delivery. A full-service department store like MB provided home delivery. An unidentified driver poses with his panel truck in 1966. (NOPL.)

Keep it cool. Joseph Bel (left) and Harvey McNab, of the building's engineering services staff, pose in front of the air-conditioning controls for MB Canal Street. They were part of a staff of six that kept the system pumping out 2,000 tons of cooling capacity. (NOPL.)

GRAND TOUR. The pipes and drums of the Black Watch (a regiment of the British Army) performed to kick off the Grand Tour of the World promotion at Canal Street in August 1967. (NOPL.)

EXECUTIVE TRANSITION. Robert Sonfield (seated, left) succeeded E.J. Jones (seated, right) as president of Maison Blanche in July 1968 on the occasion of Jones's retirement. Isidore Newman II (Isidore Newman's grandson and president of City Stores) stands over the two men. (NOPL.)

Scholarships. At right, John Bivona Sr. (left) looks on as Robert Sonfield (right) congratulates his son John Jr. on receiving a Maison Blanche–sponsored scholarship to Tulane University. Below, the scene repeats itself in 1970 as Bruce Bivona became the second member of the family to become a Maison Blanche scholar. Isidore Newman II (former president of MB and then-president of City Stores) congratulates John Sr. Both Bivona sons wear Naval Junior Reserve Officers Training Corps (NJROTC) uniforms; John Jr. graduated from St. Aloysius, and Bruce was a member of the first graduating class of Brother Martin High School. (Both, NOPL.)

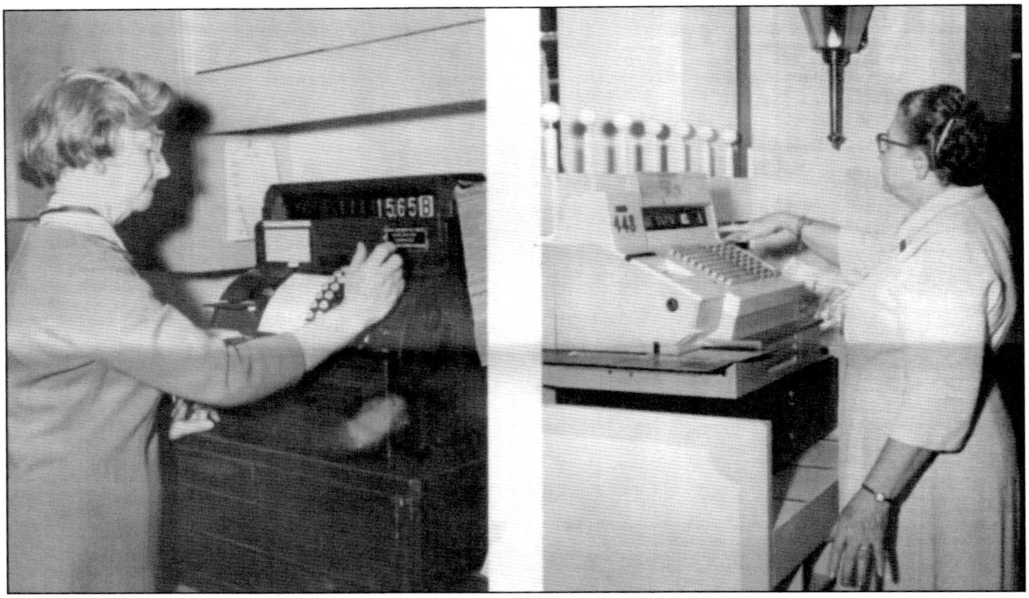

Make the Sale. Above, sales associates demonstrate using the old cash registers and their replacements implemented in the stores in 1970. At left is an assortment of the forms used by MB employees in 1970. (Both, NOPL.)

FAMILY AFFAIR. At its peak, MB was one of metro New Orleans's largest employers. Many families had two or more people working for the company in one capacity or another. The Palumbos are a good example: Mary was buyer for the bridal department in the 1970s and 1980s, and Vincent was manager of the photography studio and an occasional columnist for *Shop Talk*. (NOPL.)

CONTINUING EDUCATION. The 1967 class of the Maison Blanche School of Retailing includes, from left to right, (first row) Paula Randall, Sylvia Shushan, Carolyn Frey, Donnis Ringstaff, Penny Clarke, Mary Palumbo, Eileen Fehr, and Janet Benezech; (second row) Rosemary Bird, Mary Luce, Betty Hewett, Linda Saulny, Marcia Morgan, Antoinette King, Sheila Galiber, Lena Chisesi, and Russell Boudoin; (third row) Michael Zerlin, Casey Stuart, Donald Aguillard, Roy Riviere, Frank Madiedo, Manuel Solano, and Elsie Arcana. (NOPL.)

Helping Hands. When Hurricane Camille struck the Mississippi Gulf Coast in 1969, a team of delivery drivers and warehouse workers assembled to put together goods and materials to bring to affected areas. The team includes, from left to right, Francis Farenholt, Charles Detiveaux, George Kippers, Dominic Saragusa, David April, Raymond Cardinale, Anthony Greco, and Mike Baldini. (NOPL.)

Dining. Shown in 1970 are some of the selections at Chez Nous, the employee cafeteria in the Canal Street store. At various times, the Canal Street store operated a snack bar counter and full-service restaurant for customers, as well as the Snack Store behind the main building. (NOPL.)

Management Training. In addition to the School of Retail, Maison Blanche provided training to managers through its Supervisory Employee Relations Techniques (SERT) Phase II program. Those completing the eight-week program in 1970 are, from left to right, (first row) Kappy Pfaff, Elvira Schmitt, Bernice Emig, Grayce Dugas, Perla Harris, Sylvia Shushan, and Ruth Shepherd; (second row) Nick Morvant, Mike Ferrara, Russell Boudoin, Mike Gremillion, Paul Daigle, Claire Pearson (director of merchandise training and program coordinator), Cecil Lanier (course instructor), Imra Donnes, Tommy Balser, Rita Dranga, and Stanley Canepa. (NOPL.)

Honoring 50 Years. Felix Poche (left) receives congratulations, a watch, a diamond service pin, and a $1,000 savings bond from MB president Robert Sonfield on the occasion of his retirement on December 5, 1970. Poche started with the store as an errand boy at the age of 15. (NOPL.)

Top of the Class. Robert Sonfield, president, stands between Ann Morrison and Mike Gremillion, the valedictorians of the 1971 class of the School of Retailing. (NOPL.)

Merchandise College. MB's Merchandise College was a training program for employees on track to be managers and buyers. President Sonfield presented crests to some of those completing the program in 1971. Seen here are, from left to right, Gerald Singer, Ronnie Readman, Alphonsine Boos, Anita Bourgeois, Linda Saulny, and Sonfield. (NOPL.)

CASH REGISTER ACCURACY. In 1972, winners of the T-5-T contest measuring accuracy with class 5 registers are, from left to right, Eugie Blanchard, H.G. Kuttner (research director and contest coordinator), Gloria Uhl, Deborah Riddle, MB president Robert Sonfield, Mary Borne, Darlene Lang, E.R. Bordelon (personnel director), and Bernice Schmidt. (NOPL.)

A PART OF YOUR HISTORY!

In April of 1925 the Saenger Theater owners joined with owners of Maison Blanche to form WSMB, New Orleans first commercial radio station. Since that time the history of WSMB has been an integral part of New Orleans and the broadcast industry.

THE EARLY DAYS!

WSMB introduced New Orleans to radio entertainment and information. Live broadcasts from the Saenger theaters were combined with music and talk shows from WSMB'S Canal Street studios. *The Noonday Program, The Dinner Program, The Deluxe Program* and others were broadcast from the same studios WSMB uses today.

THE FIRST NETWORKS!

1929 saw another first for WSMB and New Orleans. The station joined the brand new NBC Red Network. NBC brought WSMB programs like: *The Lucky Strike Dance Hour, The Voice of Firestone, The Palmolive Hour, The Honeymooners*, and many other classics. The first authentic Dixieland Jazz program carried nationwide was broadcast from WSMB studios over the NBC Network.

AN FM PIONEER

WSMB became one of the first to broadcast on FM. From 1947 until 1953 WSMB AM/FM was on the air. In 1953 WSMB discontinued FM broadcasts for two reasons. One was simple, very few people had FM radios. The second reason was the birth of a new competitor, a business called *television!*

A DECADE OF CHANGES!

The 1950's were a time of change for the radio industry. Television took over the audiences for comedy and drama programs and radio began to experiment. Most stations converted to music programs and "disc-jockey" became a household word! WSMB experimented like everyone else. Listeners began hearing music programs with personality hosts. Do you remember: *The Scott Muni Show, The Sid Noel Show, Here's Pearce*, or *The Roy Roberts Show?*

THE BIRTH OF TALK RADIO!

By 1960 radio stations began to specialize. WSMB began a shift to the Personality/News/Talk station we are today. In 1961 Roy Roberts teamed up with News Director Jeff Hug to become the first "morning team". Their crazy antics quickly earned them the name "Nut and Jeff". The name stuck and today The Nut and Jeff Show is America's longest running talk show team! Another name to appear was Keith Rush. For 17 years now The Keith Rush Show from 10:00 AM to 2:00 PM has given New Orleans a chance to "talk back"!

THANK YOU!

We are proud to have been at the front of every major change in New Orleans since 1925! With your continued support, we look forward to the next 60 years together!

Trina Augusta
Earl Casey
Jeff Hug
Roy Roberts
Walter Smith
Minnette Wintering

Gene Bellau
Al Cazenave
Andre Laborde
Keith Rush
Charles Travis
Rod Wagner
Jake Fousch

Roberta Bock
Richard Fahey
Rosalie Lockhart
Randy Savoie
Jerry Valence
Terry Westerfield
Karen Gervais

Greg Brown
Jennifer Fontenot
Kirk Melancon
Don Schmidt
Dennis Williams
Bob Martin

WSMB
1350 Radio

MARKING 60 YEARS. A newspaper advertisement from 1985 marks the 60th anniversary of WSMB. A then relatively unknown talk radio pundit named Rush Limbaugh would debut in New Orleans on WSMB. Limbaugh's popularity appealed to the 50,000-watt, clear-channel WWL radio station. Unable to get the syndication rights to Limbaugh's program, WWL-AM did the next best thing: they bought WSMB and transferred the show to the more powerful station. (NOPL.)

Three

Mr. Bingle

In 1947, Emile Alline, then a window display manager at Maison Blanche, saw the Uncle Mistletoe character at a Marshall Field's store in Chicago and wanted his store to have its own special Christmas character. Alline presented the snow fairy concept to then-president of Maison Blanche, Herbert Shwartz (Simon Shwartz's son). Shwartz liked the character, naming him Mr. Bingle so that he would have a direct connection to MB. Alline wanted Mr. Bingle to be something more than just an advertising drawing. In 1948, he enlisted a French Quarter puppeteer named Edwin Harmon "Oscar" Isentrout to make the little snowman come alive. From 1948 until his death in 1985, Isentrout (who was nicknamed Oscar because a denizen of the Quarter dubbed his puppet shows "Oscar and the little woodenheads") was the voice and motion of Mr. Bingle.

Early Print Advertisements. Mr. Bingle's initial appearances were in print advertisements, such as this one from 1947. (NOPL.)

Family Collections. Since the 1950s, when Alline's prototype was turned into production models for sale, Mr. Bingle has been sold in all sorts of sizes. Jennifer Lloyd's collection ranges from the 1960s to the present. (Jennifer Lloyd.)

Outdoor Display. The big Mr. Bingle that was hung on the front of Canal Street in the 1980s was not the first large outdoor display. A large Santa and Mr. Bingle display is placed on the front of MB Canal Street for the 1952 Christmas season. (NOPL.)

GIFT CERTIFICATES. Long before the age of electronic gift cards, department stores sold paper gift certificates to shoppers stumped on what to buy for presents. Mr. Bingle helps make the sales in this early-1950s newspaper advertisement. (NOPL.)

VISITING SANTA. As much as children of all ages in New Orleans love Mr. Bingle, they still ask Santa for presents. In this 1958 photograph, Arthur Wehl gives his Christmas list to Saint Nick. (Arthur Wehl.)

FLYING INTO NOLA. In 1966 and 1967, Maison Blanche partnered with Eastern Airlines to fly in Santa and Mr. Bingle. Both Christmas characters made a grand entrance at Moisant Airport (now Louis Armstrong New Orleans International), and a motorcade then escorted them to Canal Street and the toy department. (NOPL.)

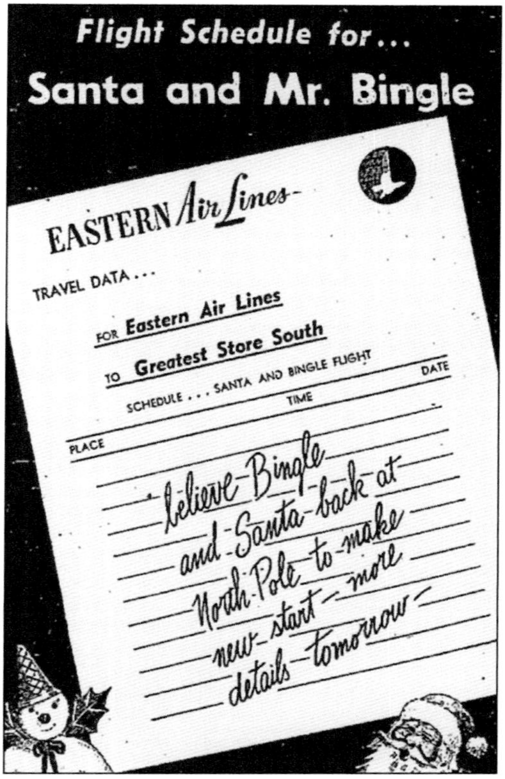

CHRISTMAS BUDDY. Andrea Kathleen Faulkner Mouritsen hugs her Mr. Bingle in the late 1970s. (Bettye Mouritsen.)

RECOMMENDED BY MR. BINGLE. The little snowman with the holly wings was everywhere in print advertisements during the holiday season, as seen in this women's clothing advertisement from 1957. (NOPL.)

CHRISTMAS MOTORCADE. This 1967 advertisement not only promotes Santa and Mr. Bingle's flight plan, it also includes a map of their motorcade from the airport in Kenner to Canal Street. In other years, Santa arrived downtown by sleigh and helicopter. (NOPL.)

Downtown Displays. As seen on page 49, the front of the Canal Street store was a regular canvas for creative Christmas displays. The image above shows the store decorated for the 1964 holiday season, and below, the new MB logo is prominently displayed on red panels in 1979. (Above, NOPL; below, Tess Conrad.)

Big-Time Bingle. While Mr. Bingle was always a prominent part of Canal Street displays, he returned to the front of the store in a large-scale format in the 1980s. (UNO.)

Modern Logo. Santa and Mr. Bingle continue to team up in print in the 1980s, along with the modern MB logo. (NOPL.)

Bookworm Bingle. Mr. Bingle pops up all over town at Christmastime, even making an appearance at the library of the Louisiana State University Medical Center. (Jennifer Lloyd.)

Derivative Bingle. Mr. Bingle's popularity inspires a number of unofficial depictions, including this one by Anthony "Turducken" DelRosario. (Anthony DelRosario.)

Bingle Gras! Mr. Bingle often makes unofficial appearances during New Orleans's other big celebration, Mardi Gras. At left, a member of the Phunny Phorty Phellows masks as Mr. Bingle for the krewe's streetcar ride on Twelfth Night in 2008. Below, a Mr. Bingle masker poses with a Stormtrooper in the French Quarter in 2011. (Left, Carlos "Infrogmation" May; below, Joe Hollier.)

Jingle, Jangle, Jingle. "Here comes Mister Bingle"—the lyrics to the *Mr. Bingle Jingle* on WDSU-TV are a fond memory to many New Orleanians. Unfortunately, many people get them wrong, and one reader of the *Gambit* turned to the paper's history trivia columnist, "Blake Pontchartrain," for an authoritative answer in the 1990s. (NOPL.)

Icons. Photographer Christopher Porche West captures two classic NOLA icons in one shot—Mr. Bingle presiding over Canal Street and the mule-drawn Roman Candy wagon—in the early 1980s. (Christopher Porche West.)

NATIVITY. While Mr. Bingle was the official Christmas ambassador of Maison Blanche, the company did not forget the serious side of the holiday season, as evidenced by this front-window Nativity display in 1966. (NOPL.)

"OSCAR." Emile Alline hired puppeteer Edwin Harmon "Oscar" Isentrout in 1947 to give Mr. Bingle movement and a voice. So popular was Oscar's presentation of Mr. Bingle that the store hired him to do numerous public appearances with the puppet, including live television spots on WDSU-TV in the 1960s. In this photograph from the store's Grand Tour sales promotion in 1967, Oscar is displaying a puppet of a French girl. (NOPL.)

CUSTOMIZED BINGLES. Many Mr. Bingle dolls take on traits of their owners. Here is George "Loki" Williams's Mr. Bingle, proudly displaying a promotional button for NewOrleans.com. (George "Loki" Williams IV.)

The Bingle Puppets. Emile Alline commissioned two marionettes of Mr. Bingle for Oscar to use. One of those puppets came into the possession of Jeffery Kent after Oscar passed away. The puppet was severely damaged by Hurricane Katrina, but Kent painstakingly restored Mr. Bingle to his original condition. Since local television weatherman Bob Breck encouraged Kent to take on the project, Breck reintroduced Mr. Bingle to New Orleans on his show. (Jeffery Kent.)

Mr. Bingle Silenced. Oscar Isentrout passed away on July 25, 1985. He was buried in an unmarked grave at Hebrew Rest Cemetery in Gentilly. In 2005, author Sean Patrick Doles wrote a novel telling the fictional tale of *Saving Mr. Bingle* and led a fundraising drive to purchase and install a headstone on Oscar's grave. (Author.)

Mr. Bingle Visits Oscar. Jeffrey Kent photographed the restored Mr. Bingle marionette visiting his voice. (Jeffery Kent.)

Leaving Canal Street. The big Mr. Bingle was placed into storage and remained there until 2005 (with the exception of one brief appearance at the Dillard's store at Lakeside Mall in Metairie). At that time, Dillard's donated Mr. Bingle to the Friends of City Park, who paid to have the figure refurbished. Mr. Bingle made his debut at City Park's "Celebration in the Oaks" light display in November 2005, giving the city a much needed morale boost in a rough year. (Louis Maistros.)

Four

Fashion and Advertising through the Years

The public persona of a department store includes, among other things, its storefronts, the employees, and the store's merchandise. Additionally, the impression the store's various advertising campaigns leave on shoppers is critical. Beginning with print advertising, mostly in local newspapers, Maison Blanche quickly established its Greatest Store South brand. As radio became popular, MB took advertising in that medium to another level, partnering with the Saenger Theater to purchase their own radio station, WSMB. From the time the station went on the air in 1925 until the time the chain ceased operations, the simple act of station identification was advertising. While MB did not move into ownership in television, the popularity of Oscar Isentrout's live commercials with his Mr. Bingle puppet firmly established the store's brand on the small screen. The management and merchandise buyers of Maison Blanche prided themselves in offering quality items that ranged from fashionable to practical. In addition to the many other departments in the stores, MB was the go-to place for Boy Scout and Girl Scout uniforms and accessories.

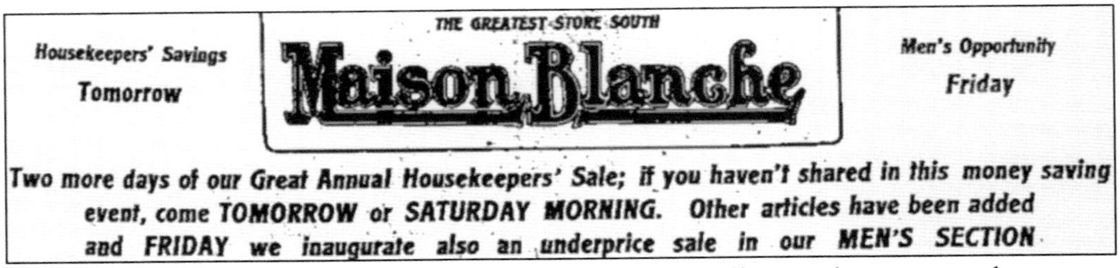
THE GREATEST STORE SOUTH

Maison Blanche

Housekeepers' Savings
Tomorrow

Men's Opportunity
Friday

Two more days of our Great Annual Housekeepers' Sale; if you haven't shared in this money saving event, come TOMORROW or SATURDAY MORNING. Other articles have been added and FRIDAY we inaugurate also an underprice sale in our MEN'S SECTION.

ADVERTISING FROM 1908. This newspaper advertisement is offering sales to entice shoppers to go downtown. The "Housekeepers' " sale was the forerunner of the citywide Community Bargain Days sales of the 1960s and 1970s. (NOPL.)

NEW LOGO, 1968. Maison Blanche unveils the store's new logo on the cover of the *Shop Talk* employee newsletter in November 1968. (NOPL.)

AUDIO-VISUAL. Above, sales associate Sarah McFarland inspects Canal Street's selection of portable television sets in 1967. McFarland promoted the United Way's Fair Share fundraising campaign as "Miss Fair Chere." To the right is a 1920s advertisement for phonographs sold in the store's music salon. (Both, NOPL.)

MB IN 1915. Above, merchandise is on display on the first floor of MB Canal Street in 1915. Below is an advertisement from the same period, proudly touting the store's imported goods. (Both, NOPL.)

ANNIVERSARY SALE. The store's anniversary was a big deal in terms of sales promotions. Being a summer event, contests for employees, parties, talent shows, and other festivities all motivated the staff during the dog days of summer. This 1925 advertisement shows the WSMB transmission towers now mounted atop the building. (NOPL.)

Private Labels. This is a paper-doll promotional advertisement from the back cover of the *Shop Talk* employee newsletter of February 1972. Maison Blanche, through City Stores, had excellent buying power that enabled the department store chains to get private-label runs from manufacturers. (NOPL.)

For the Gentlemen. Above is the men's department in 1967. Below, men's sportswear buyer Rick Lauer (left) and men's furnishings buyer Arnold Reuben display some of the private-label merchandise they have acquired for the store's 1967 Fathers' Day sale. (Both, NOPL.)

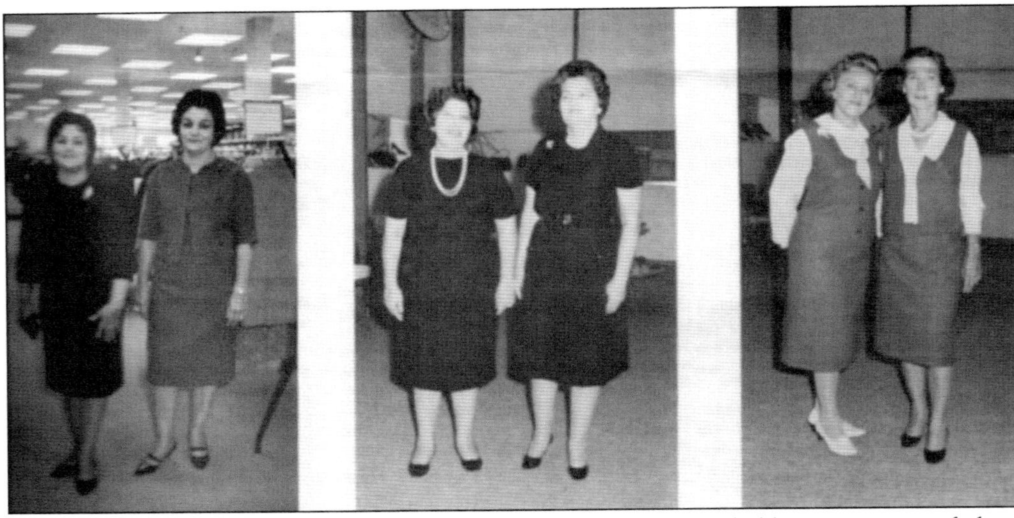

DRESSES FOR $10! Salespeople from the first floor of Canal Street held an impromptu fashion show in August 1964. Their challenge was to buy a dress from either the main store or the Budget Annex that met employee dress standards but was still less than or equal to $10. (NOPL.)

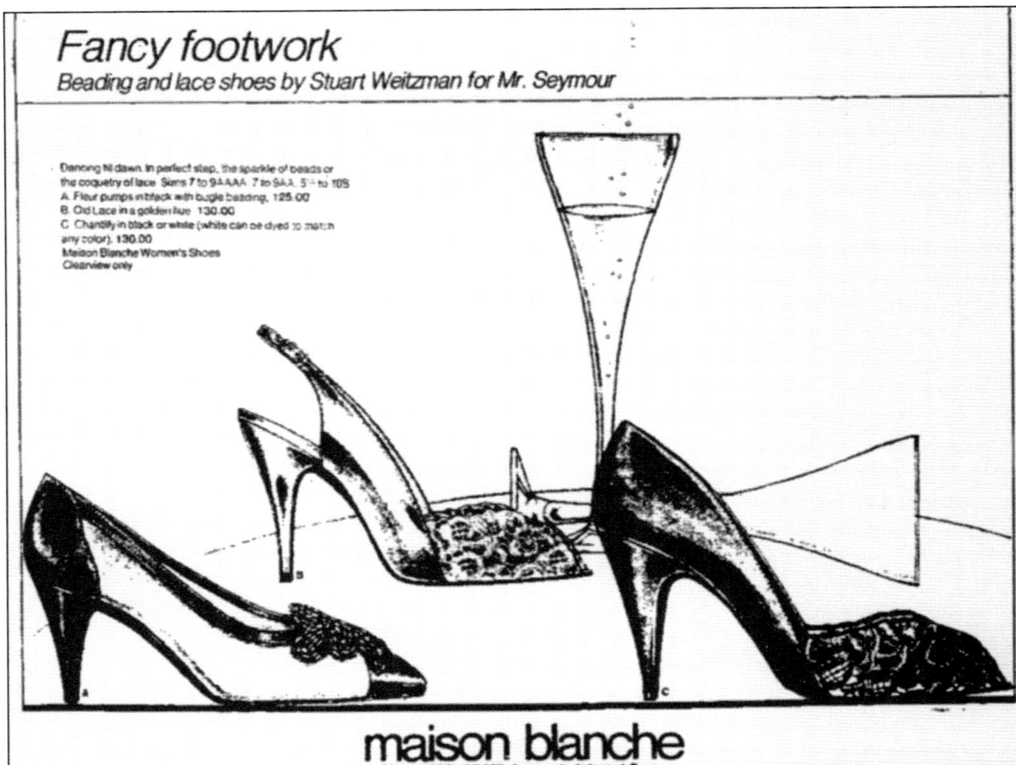

SHOES! The shoes in this 1970s advertisement are not very sensible in terms of matching the $10 dresses, but they are still good-looking. (NOPL.)

Bridal. Maison Blanche was one of the premier stores in New Orleans for brides. Registering at MB was a must. To encourage that, the store held one or more bridal shows annually. This is an invitation to one of these events held at the Royal Orleans Hotel (now the Omni Royal Orleans) a few blocks away in the French Quarter in the 1970s. (Both, NOPL.)

MAISON BLANCHE

Bridal Fashion Show

2:00 p.m. Saturday, March twenty-fifth

GRAND SALON, ROYAL ORLEANS HOTEL

Admit Two

DOS AND DON'TS. Maxine Alagar (far left) models a minidress that was acceptable for employees to wear in 1970, while Paulette Sauls's striped shorts will likely get her sent home. Margarite Fischer's black dress and colorful scarf (second from right) are a striking contrast to Lillian Lloyd's loud, print dress and long beads, demonstrating just about everything wrong for a female sales associate to do. (NOPL.)

WINTER FASHION. This fashionable outfit from 1970 would be acceptable for employee wear, but its price tag may have put it out of the average sales associate's budget. (NOPL.)

WHO DAT! In 1967, Maison Blanche signed New Orleans Saints linebacker Steve Stonebreaker to a promotional contract. Stonebreaker made numerous public appearances for the store, such as this Ladies' Day appearance in 1969, as well as posing for advertisements. Stonebreaker was one of the original Saints, playing for the team in its first season (1967). (Both, NOPL.)

Cocktails, Fashion, and Jazz. Capitalizing on a credit-card base spanning decades, MB often invited account holders to special events via direct mail, like this 1983 flyer for an evening of entertainment. (NOPL.)

Scents and Summer Wear. Above is a shot of the fragrance counter on the first floor in 1964. A nice, light cologne would be an excellent accessory for the breezy dress advertised (at right) in 1982. (Both, NOPL.)

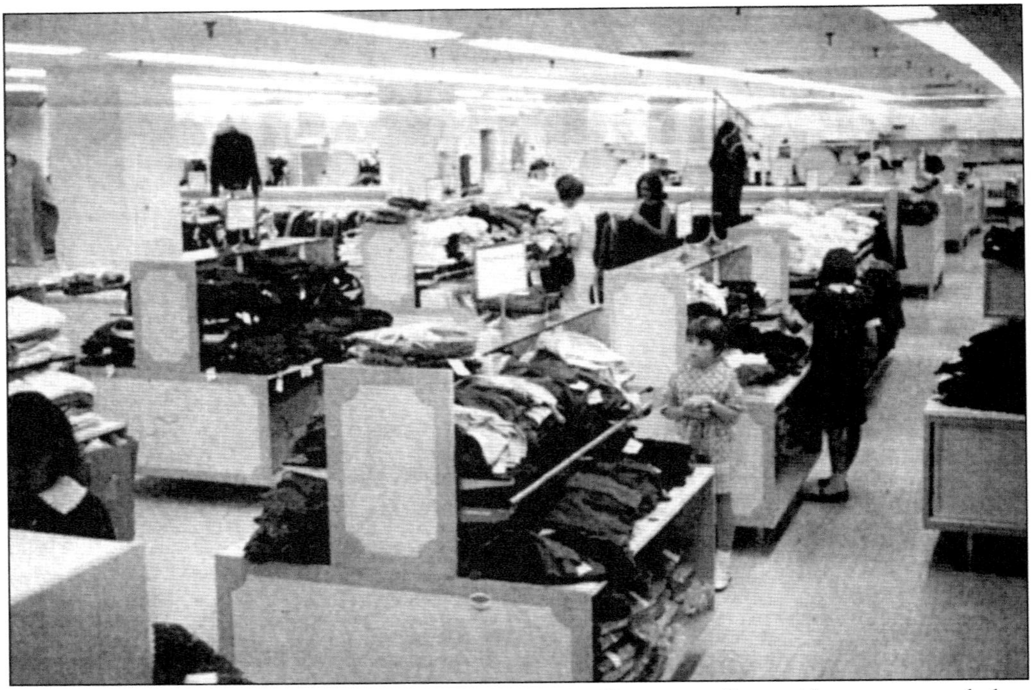

GIRLS AND BOYS. Above, a young lady checks out the fashions in the girls' department in 1966. At left, classic khaki is the look for boys going back to school in 1969. (Both, NOPL.)

HOUSEWARES. This *American Modern* advertisement from the 1950s shows just some of the extensive merchandise the store carried in the housewares department. (NOPL.)

MORE EMPLOYEE FASHION. The well-dressed sales associate in 1964 could easily find fashionable clothes to wear to work in the budget departments, as these unidentified models demonstrate. (NOPL.)

Fine Jewelry. While Maison Blanche sold costume jewelry for years, the store did not open a fine jewelry department until 1963, as seen above. Below, a shopper checks out the fine jewelry in 1966. (Both, NOPL.)

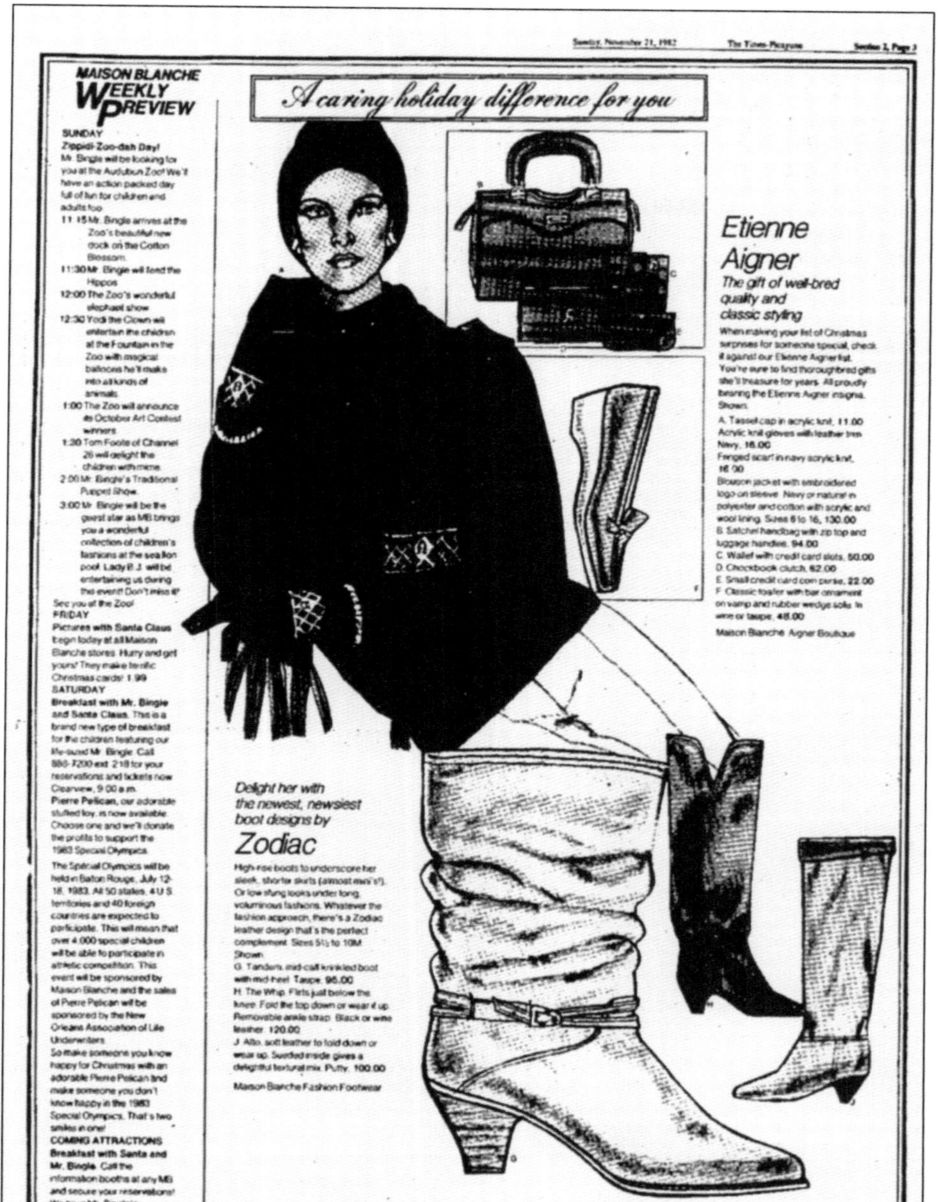

BOOTS MADE FOR WALKING. This 1982 holiday-season advertisement touts the Etienne Aigner line of boots and leather accessories for women. The left-hand column of the *Times-Picayune* newspaper lists various Mr. Bingle appearances and other store-sponsored holiday activities. (NOPL.)

Sports Sponsorships. Not all advertising was in the newspaper and on television. These Hayne S. Ragas photographs for the New Orleans Recreation Department (NORD) show a Maison Blanche–sponsored NORD playground-league baseball team. At left, team captains and managers pose for Ragas. Below, the team receives awards and congratulations from NORD officials and MB representatives. (Both, NOPL.)

Runway Leaders. Part of Maison Blanche's support of the arts in New Orleans included annually hosting activities during the Overture to the Cultural Season. The store presented the Rex Award to world-class fashion designers at a fashion show and dinner. This was the program cover for the 1976 soirée. (NOPL.)

HEADING EAST. Two Canal Street employees display Japanese silk jackets for the 1967 Grand Tour promotion. (NOPL.)

FURNITURE. MB was one of the best places to shop for furniture and other home furnishings, as is evidenced by this 1968 photograph. (NOPL.)

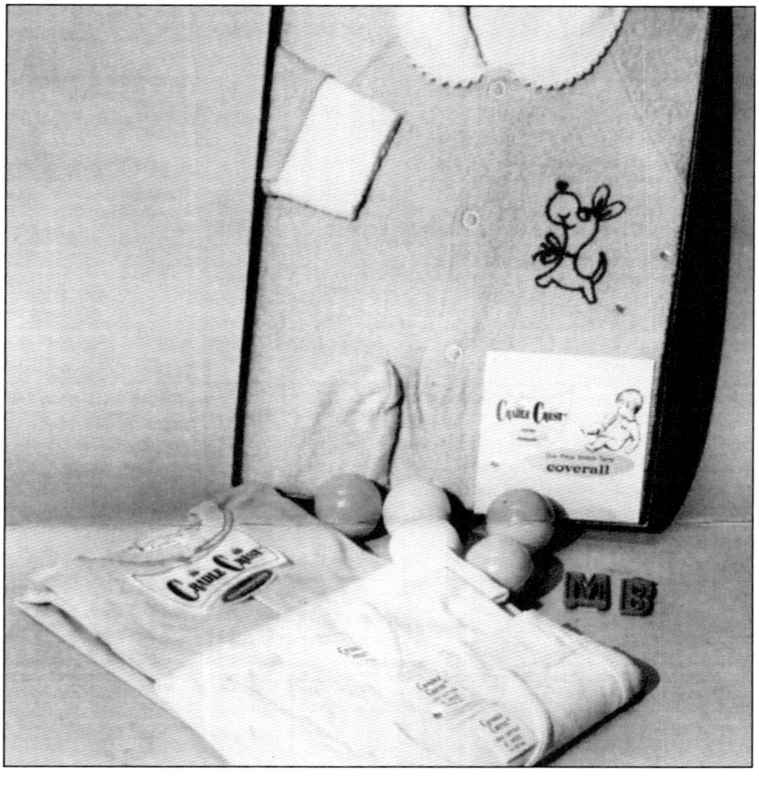

KIDS' STUFF. Here are some items from the infant's department in 1970. (NOPL.)

CLOSING TIME. This direct mail from 1986 is promoting one of the last events held at the Canal Street store, which featured an appearance by designer Tommy Hilfiger. (NOPL.)

Five

Suburban Expansion

Like most of the store's history, Maison Blanche's development beyond Canal Street reflected the growth of the city as a whole. The postwar housing boom created new residential subdivisions in Gentilly, Mid City, and Lakeview. MB acted on those opportunities, opening new stores in Gentilly and Mid City in the late 1940s, Metairie and the West Bank in the 1950s, and in shopping malls in the 1960s and 1970s. By 1975, the chain had stores easily accessible to all parts of the Tri-Parish area, as well as a store up the river, in Baton Rouge, Louisiana. While the expansion of Maison Blanche into the suburbs kept the chain alive and growing, the general trend of shopping in the suburbs rather than downtown meant the importance of the main store on Canal Street began to decline. Executive management and the merchandise buyers may have still operated out of Canal, but the sales were coming from Metairie (Clearview) and New Orleans East (Lake Forest). The suburban malls continued to make Maison Blanche the Greatest Store South.

POSTWAR GROWTH. Following World War II, New Orleans experienced the baby boom, like other parts of the country. The demand for new housing grew, and subdivisions, like Pontchartrain Park, were developed. (NOPL.)

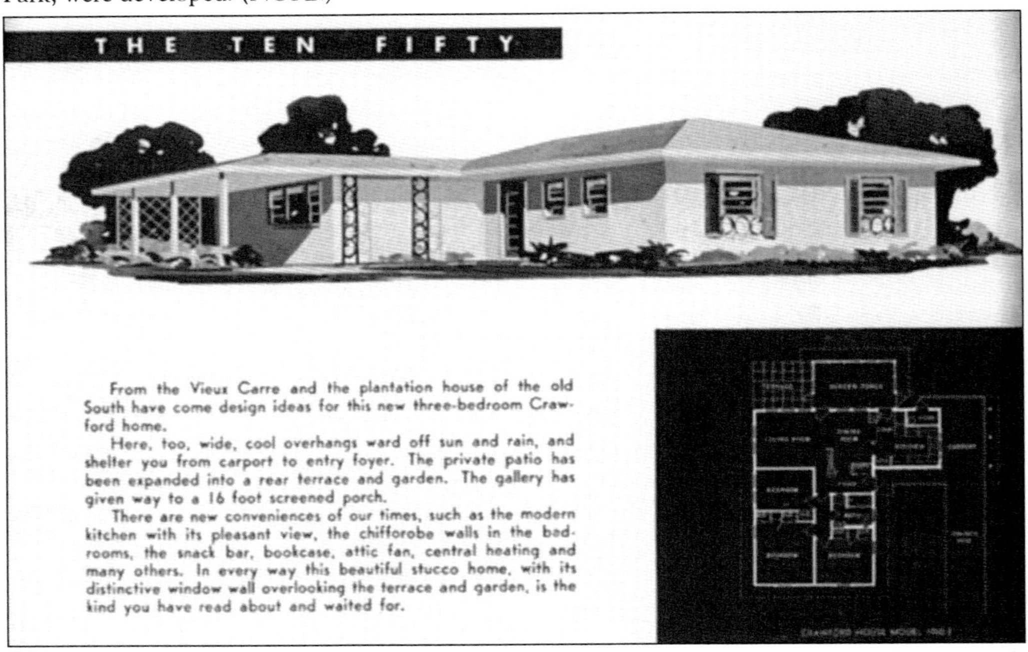

SUBURBS IN THE CITY. South of Pontchartrain Park was the Gentilly Woods subdivision with its affordable, suburban-style homes. The combination of these two subdivisions increased the opportunities for retail development. Maison Blanche recognized this opportunity, opening a larger store on Gentilly Boulevard. (NOPL.)

"A Complete Suburban Department Store." That was the proud boast of Maison Blanche on September 12, 1947, as the company announced the opening of its second suburban location, on Gentilly Boulevard near Elysian Fields Avenue. Below is the building today. When MB opened a store down the street in Gentilly Woods Shopping Center, MB Gentilly became a budget store. It then became a pizza restaurant after City Stores sold the property. Now it is an automobile parts store. (Both, NOPL.)

Tulane and Carrollton. Maison Blanche continued the chain's expansion in 1947 with the opening of the Carrollton store. Above is the MB Carrollton in 1950. Like MB Gentilly, this store was converted to a budget store when the large, suburban malls opened. Below is the building today. (Mid-City Lanes, "Home of Rock 'n' Bowl," moved to a new location farther up Carrollton Avenue in 2009.) (Above, NOPL; below, author.)

WESTWARD GROWTH. The city's decision to fill in the navigable waterway to Lake Pontchartrain, the New Basin Canal, made it easier to get to the western suburb of Metairie. This aerial photograph shows the Carrollton Interchange under construction. MB's Carrollton store is across the street from the baseball stadium (Pelican Field) in the foreground. (NOPL.)

JEFFERSON PARISH. With the Carrollton Interchange making it easier to get up Airline Highway, Maison Blanche moved out to Jefferson Parish, opening the Airline Village store. Located along the highway that connected New Orleans to Baton Rouge (US 61), it serviced the Metairie neighborhood. This was the newspaper announcement for the opening of the Airline Village store on March 3, 1957. (NOPL.)

Airline Village. The Airline Village store underwent major renovations in the spring of 1971. With its rear parking lot easily accessible to Old Metairie, the store continued to be popular. Above is the exterior of the store in July 1971. Below is a ladies casual-wear department after the renovations. (Both, NOPL.)

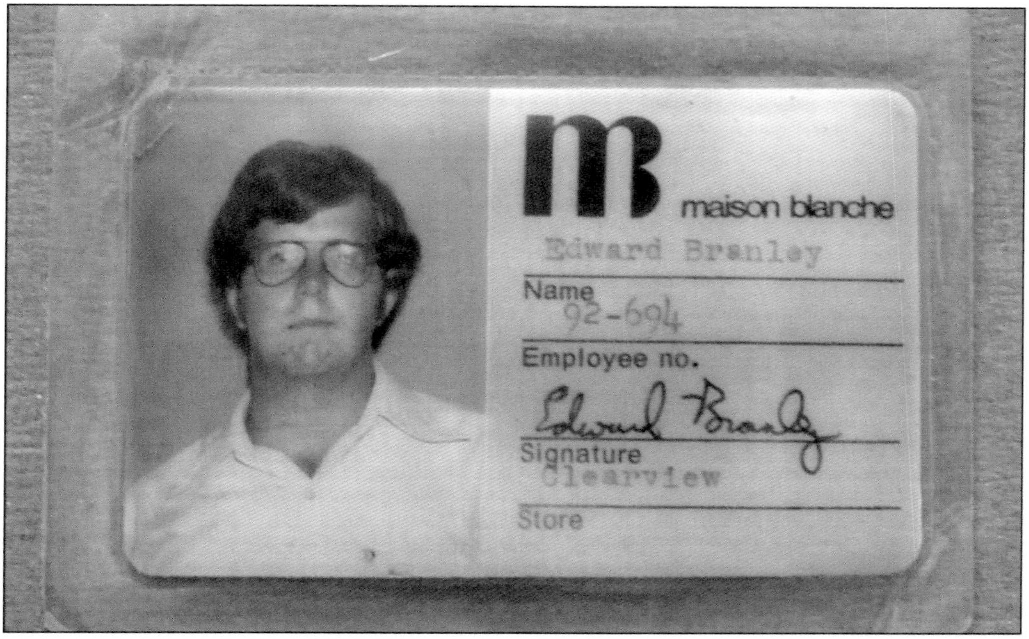

Employee Credentials. While there was no need for extensive security at the stores, each employee was still issued an identification card. These were used most often when entering or leaving the stores outside of scheduled hours, as well as to make purchases using the employee discount offered by the store. (Author.)

Sporting Goods. Bicycles and other sports items are on display at Airline Village store in July 1971. (NOPL.)

London Britches. Jeans and other casual wear are displayed at Airline Village store in July 1971. (NOPL.)

Airline Village Today. The Airline Village store was closed in the 1970s, after Maison Blanche Clearview opened. The property was acquired by an Assembly of God congregation, which then sold it to the current owners, a nondenominational Christian congregation. (Author.)

CROSSING THE RIVER. Maison Blanche expanded to Westside Shopping Center in Gretna, on the west bank of the Mississippi River, in 1958. The original store underwent extensive expansion and renovation, beginning in the summer of 1968, which doubled the floor space. The expansion allowed MB to open a budget store in Westside at that time. (NOPL.)

REMAINING OPEN. Like Canal Street in the mid-1900s, Westside stayed open during remodeling construction so employees could continue to work and the store continue to profit, as seen here in the shoe department. (NOPL.)

The New Westside. Shown here is the cover of *Shop Talk* in February 1970, offering a preview of the expanded store. (NOPL.)

Eastern Expansion. Maison Blanche moved the Gentilly store down the street in 1961. This is an aerial view of Gentilly Woods Shopping Center in 1968. Maison Blanche is the left-side anchor; Sears anchors the right side. (NOPL.)

In-Store Demonstrations. In addition to special promotions, artisans occasionally offered demonstrations of their crafts. In July 1972, James Hussey demonstrates how he creates the very popular decoupage handbags sold at MB stores. (NOPL.)

GENTILLY WOODS TODAY. The building that was once MB Gentilly Woods was acquired by the shopping center's next-door neighbor, the New Orleans Baptist Theological Seminary, which now uses it for a number of purposes, including classrooms and a Christian bookstore. (Author.)

Metairie Mall. Above is Maison Blanche Clearview under construction in June 1968. The mall spans the area on Clearview Parkway (foreground) from Veterans Boulevard to Interstate 10. (NOPL.)

CHRISTMAS EVE. Rebecca Lester Ventura (left) and Tiffany Finnorn Schielder pose in the cosmetics department at the Clearview store during a lull in one of the last Maison Blanche Christmas seasons during the mid-1990s. (Rebecca Lester Ventura.)

HOME FURNISHINGS. Everything needed to make any Metairie home beautiful was available at the Airline Village store in 1971. (NOPL.)

OPEN FOR BUSINESS. Shown here is the completed Clearview store a year later, in June 1969. (NOPL.)

TOP PERFORMERS. Clearview sales associates receiving 100 percent shopper reports in January 1970 are, from left to right, Nelly Sullivan, Claire Patterson, Dorothy Lemoine, and Beverly Lopez. (NOPL.)

Suburban Events. Sales associates Rebecca Lester Ventura (left) and Robin Boling pose during a charity event held at the store in the mid-1990s. (Rebecca Lester Ventura.)

Celebration! Veteran sales specialist Thomas Youngblood is serving cake during one of the parties held in the staff break room. (Rebecca Lester Ventura.)

Modern Mall. Maison Blanche Clearview was one of the first stores closed when the chain was sold to Dillard's in the mid-1990s, as Dillard's operates a three-floor store in Lakeside Mall. The owners of Clearview Mall revamped their property, bringing in a 12-screen AMC theater and several restaurants to support the theater. The MB space was leased to Target. (Author.)

CONVERSION. Compare this view of Target, which now anchors Clearview Mall's western side, with the photograph on page 103. Target only uses two of the building's three floors for retail, leasing the top floor as office space. (Author.)

MOVING EAST. This is the corner of Alvar Street and Almonaster Boulevard in Gentilly in 1972, before construction began on the warehouse. When the city expanded Almonaster Boulevard, using it to link Claiborne Avenue with Gentilly Boulevard, cheaper real estate prices in lower Gentilly made projects like the new MB warehouse attractive. (NOPL.)

"Ex-it Louisa Street, Off Eye-Ten." That memorable line gave television viewers directions to years of Maison Blanche warehouse sales. Shown here is an advertisement for a sale in 1978, including a map to the warehouse. (NOPL.)

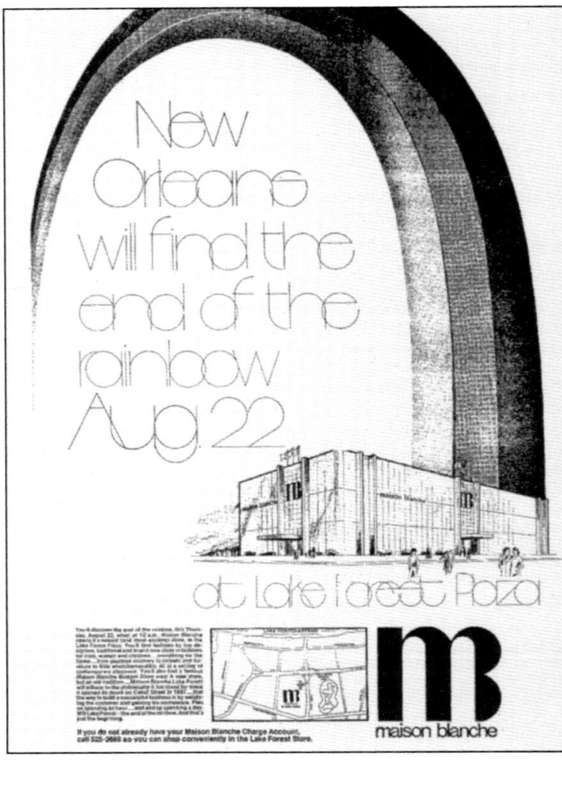

New Orleans East. The final expansion by Maison Blanche in metro New Orleans was the store in Lake Forest Plaza, which opened in 1974. The company closed Gentilly Woods at the same time. MB ventured beyond New Orleans in 1975 with the opening of a store in Bon Marche Mall in Baton Rouge. When MB was acquired by Dillard's in 1998, that chain had already closed its Lake Forest store. Dillard's opted to resume operations in New Orleans East by transitioning the MB store. The plaza was destroyed by Hurricane Katrina in 2005; what remained was demolished in 2006. (NOPL.)

Six

Puttin' on the Ritz

The flagship store on Canal Street became a branch store of Goudchaux's–Maison Blanche when it was reopened in 1984 and continued to operate until closed by Dillard's in 1998. The building was sold in 1997 to the Whitecastle development group, which included Stewart Juneau, Bill Hindman, Bernard Mason, and Rick Hodges. The group also acquired the S.H. Kress building next door, and the decision was made to convert both buildings into a hotel. The Ritz-Carlton chain was contracted to operate the new 700-plus-room hotel (including over 200 suites) and its 35,000 square feet of meeting space. The Ritz-Carlton, New Orleans, held its grand opening on October 6, 2000. The hotel was heavily damaged during Hurricane Katrina: street flooding inundated the first floor and basement, knocking out the building's electrical systems and other facilities. After $106 million was spent on repairs, the hotel reopened on December 4, 2006.

Department Store as Hotel. With 707 guest rooms, a luxurious club-level room, and extensive conference and banquet facilities, the Ritz-Carlton Hotel in New Orleans is a major player in the New Orleans tourism industry. (Author.)

Joining Buildings. The Ritz consists of both the old S.H. Kress building and the Maison Blanche building. (Author.)

KRESS. The S.H. Kress building was constructed in 1911 and completed in 1912. As part of the Ritz, the ground floor is the hotel's automobile entrance. (Author.)

CANAL STREET. The hustle and bustle of Canal Street has changed little over the years. While streetcars took a hiatus for 40 years, they returned in a more modern version with red-livery Carrollton cars in 2004. (Author.)

Closed Corner. While the corner of Canal Street and Rue Dauphine was the main entrance of the Maison Blanche store on Canal Street, the entrance to the MB office building was on the other end, next to S.H. Kress. (Author.)

FRONT DOOR. The office building portal is now the main entrance to the Ritz. (Author.)

Budget Annex. The building directly behind MB Canal Street on Rue Iberville was the store's Budget Annex. While there are two storefronts in the building on the corner of Rue Iberville and Rue Dauphine, the vast bulk of the building, with its main entrance shown here on Rue Burgundy and Rue Iberville, has been vacant for years. (Author.)

Storefronts. A Carrollton car operated by New Orleans Regional Transit Authority is about to pass in front of the Canal Street side of the Ritz. What were once the first-floor display windows of Maison Blanche are now a retail shopping area the hotel is developing. (Author.)

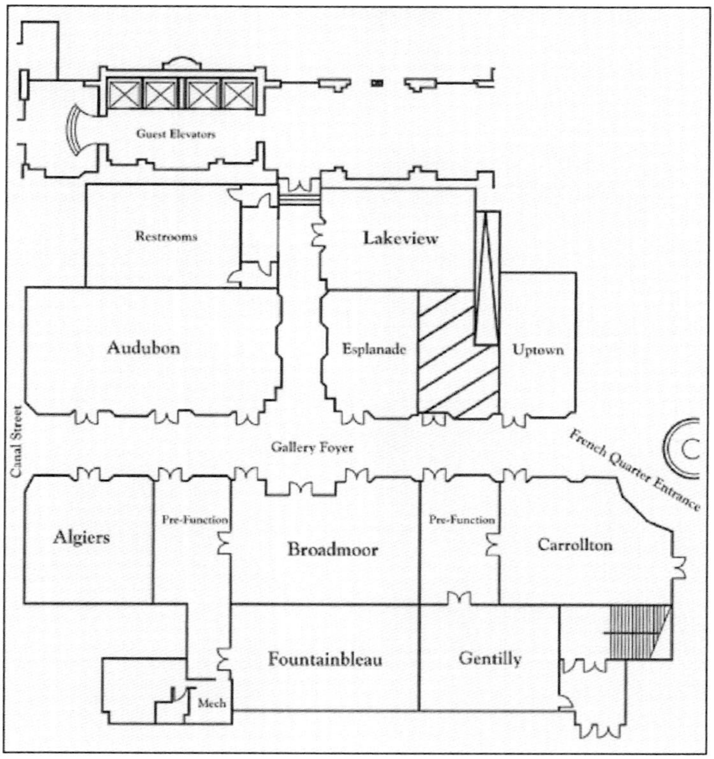

Retail to Conferences. The plan of the first floor of the Ritz shows the various conference facilities. (Author.)

Iberville to Canal. This fourth-floor hallway runs the length of the block along Rue Dauphine, from Rue Iberville to Canal Street. (Author.)

Breakfast. Shown is the continental breakfast buffet in the Maison Orleans suites, the "club" section of the Ritz. (Author.)

Relaxation. The lounge on the fourth floor is a nice place for club-level guests to enjoy quiet time. (Both, author.)

GHOSTS? The staff on the club level at the Ritz-Carlton likes to tell ghost stories about these two young ladies, but very few tales ever came out of MB in almost 90 years of retail operations. (Author.)

Meeting Place. This lovely fountain on the first floor makes for a very photogenic spot. (Author.)

Fresh Air. Shown are two views of the third-floor patio area located between the two office towers. The hardworking staff moves quickly to bring food and beverages from the Davenport Lounge to guests using the patio. (Both, author.)

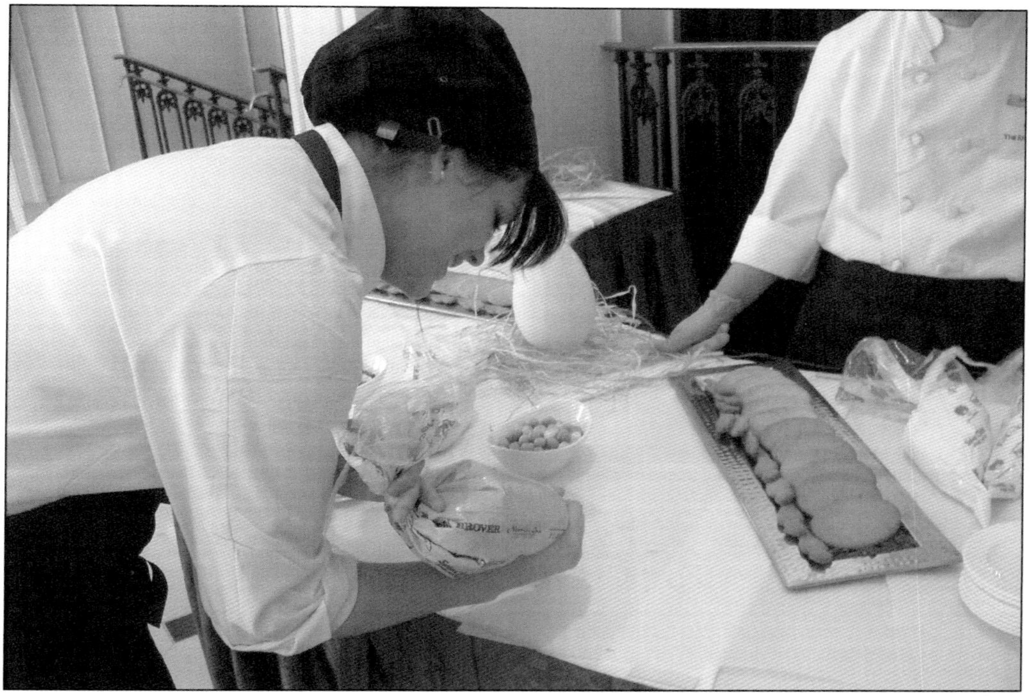

EASTER. An unidentified member of the staff practices decorating egg-shaped cookies in advance of holiday festivities for the children of hotel guests. (Author.)

BRUNCH. Here, Sunday brunch in the Davenport Lounge on the third floor is accompanied by the musical stylings of a local harpist. (Author.)

LOOKING UP. Here is a view from Rue Dauphine of what was the rear office tower. (Author.)

Rue Iberville. At the corner of Rue Dauphine and Rue Iberville is another entrance to the hotel. Prior to the 1958 extension project, the building that housed the MB Snack Store sat on this corner. (Author.)

Extended Building. Here are two views of the 1958 extension of Maison Blanche, now the Maison Orleans. (Both, author.)

BUDGET ANNEX. The footbridge over Rue Iberville, which joins the 1958 extension to the Budget Annex on the other side of the street, still remains. (Author.)

AUTOMOBILE ENTRANCE. Guests with automobiles who are staying in the Maison Orleans club rooms have their own drop-off and pick-up point on Rue Iberville. (Author.)

A Decade of the Ritz. Since its grand opening in 2000, the city has experienced quite a roller-coaster ride. Reinventing itself after the oil bust of the 1980s, the city's tourism industry reached an exciting level with the growth of its convention business and the return of streetcars to Canal Street in 2004. In 2005, Hurricane Katrina removed a lot of the luster of those accomplishments, but, like the Mardi Gras Indians, New Orleans "won't bow down . . . don't know how." (Author.)

Bibliography

Departmentstoremuseum.blogspot.com
Laborde, Peggy Scott, and John Magil. *Canal Street: New Orleans Great Wide Way*. New Orleans: Pelican Publishing, 2006.
Massa, Dominic. *New Orleans Television*. Charleston, SC: Arcadia Publishing, 2008.
Widmer, Mary Lou, and Moon Landrieu. *New Orleans 1900 to 1920*. New Orleans: Pelican Publishing, 2007.
Widmer, Mary Lou. *New Orleans in the 1920s*. New Orleans: Pelican Publishing, 1993.
www.cs.uiuc.edu/~friedman/canal/canal.htm